Birth/Brother/Breach

I was born February 16, 1952. ~~...~~ At least that's what the birth certificate says. Personally, I think they should say a little bit more than that since it is the beginning of a person's life here on planet Earth. That's a pretty important event. I am the middle child of my mother's three children who lived beyond the first day a birth. I mention tis because there was at least one before me and one after me. My parents separated when I was around 2 years old. They never lived together again.

Momma had a lot of problems with my brother who was the oldest. He was a hard worker and very caring. However, he was homosexual and very unhappy. The lifestyle was not one to be desired in the 50's, 60's, and 70's. He was a tall, lean, dark handsome gay man in a poor neighborhood being raised by a single mom in the deep south. It took a lot of attention away from the regular day to day stuff most families deal with. Every day was a new adventure with him around. We never knew what kind of trouble he would get into or even if he would be coming home from one day to the next. He might just go to work in the morning and we might not see him again for weeks at a time. Momma ended up sending him bus fare many times to get him home and just to know he was alright.

Then, there was the child who had Momma's heart. The Baby. My little sister. I believe my mother genuinely loved all of us. The difference (I think) was in how she felt about our fathers (we each had different dads). Momma always told me that my daddy had a problem with working. He didn't like it. She said he was downright lazy. I don't know much about my brother's dad. Anyway, my brother was 8 years older than me and I was 6 years older than my sister. Momma was head over heels, totally in love with my sister's father. He was about as abusive as they come but she really loved him. That love transferred over to my sister who looks almost like a carbon copy of her father. My brother and I saw it the way it really was and understood she was the preferred child. End of discussion.

Then there was yours truly – me! I was about as homely as they come. I fluctuated between pudgy and fluffy for a number of years, then I finally found skinny. I went from homely to 'you'll do in a pinch'. Momma plainly did not have a lot of time to devote to the quiet middle child. She was extremely preoccupied with the other two. Besides, she had some personal issues she was dealing with and that just didn't leave room for my growing mountain of baggage. That in itself created a bit of a breach between me and my sister. The breach never really closed but that's another story.

I'd have to say that my brother and I were closer because our personalities were somewhat similar (to a degree). He was very sensitive and giving. He never forgot a birthday or any holiday for that matter. We didn't really get to know each other as well as I wish we had. He died of cancer in 1981. He was 37 years old. My sister and I were both grown at the time. We were in what's called a backslidden state. That was horrible, horrible feeling. Just when my brother needed someone to witness to him about Jesus, my life was too tainted, too marred because of my inconsistent walk with Jesus Christ.

By that time, I was already married to husband #2 and all three of my biological daughters had been born. Let's go back a bit. Husband #1 was a good looking, womanizer, heavy drinker, and wife beater. I met him when I was 17. We got married when I was 18, and my oldest daughter (our only child together) was born shortly after my 19th birthday. He was 11 years my senior and knew his way around the block and back. I, on the other hand, didn't even know where the block was. He and I fought our way up and down the east coast. We lived on migrant camps, in cheap housing units, and in his trucks. He was a contractor who hired farm laborers for fruit and vegetable harvesting. Basically, he bought, harvested, and sold the produce for profit.

He made a really good living. Most of the time, I worked alongside him or made sure the books were in order. The lifestyle just got real old – dodging bullets, avoiding his fists, dealing with the outside women, throwing dishes or pots and pans. I'd finally had enough of him and the violence so I left him for good. After all, he had been my way out of an unhappy home *(I thought)*. It was really just a trade off from one hell hole into one of a different kind. We didn't get divorced right away but there was a definite separation.

Hello, Husband #2 & Whoredom

Then, I met this new guy. Heavy drinking, hardworking man. (Notice a pattern starting here?) He was strange but paid me a lot of attention. I was lonely and he fit the bill... for the moment. One problem, though. He was already married and had kids from his current wife (there were at least two more children from a previous relationship). By the time I figured out the futility of that affair, my second baby girl (baby #2) was already on the way. So far, husbands and boyfriends were not among my better choices. I just didn't have the skills or the experience to select well.

Shortly after my second daughter was born, I met another man. Handsome, he had a job, said the right things at the right time, and *(again)* I listened. He had been married once but was divorced. His ex-wife and two children lived out of state. OKAY! This seemed a lot better to me. No wife. Kids out of town. He was working a well-paying job. So, I went ahead and got a divorce from husband #1. This fellow and I got married. Mind you, now, this guy was working a full time, well-paying job when we got married. Unless the weather was inclement, he worked a lot. However, after we got married, I discovered he thought so much of his skill that when work was slow, he wouldn't take a minimum wage job. I kid you not! My third and last child, another little girl, was born by now.

It was during this time that I found out how much he really enjoyed marijuana, outside women, and time with 'the boys'. You know, in retrospect, I think about the day we got married. Some of our friends were throwing rice at us and one of Momma's friends said: "You'd better save that rice. You're going to need it." She meant we'd need it for food. Naturally, I was insulted when she said it but I have to admit, she was right and the time did come when we could have used it. What if I had listened to all of the warning signs BEFORE we got married? I suppose we'll never know because that window of opportunity has closed.

Alright, so now I have three little girls all born between 1971 and 1974. WHEW! I have a husband who has: a problem with working, a drug habit, and is a skirt chaser. It was during this period that I had my first encounter with Jesus.

I had always worked two or three jobs while trying to get some college credits. I was raised to believe you could never depend on anyone else, especially a man. If a job needed doing, do it yourself because people (specifically men) would always fail and disappoint you. At the most critical times, you'd find people letting you down and offering excuses instead of the promised results. This wasn't something said directly to me (at least I don't remember it being direct) but more so by watching the lives of others. I was able to listen to many adult conversations while growing up. We were raised in the south mostly but worked and traveled on a lot of migrant labor camps in the northeastern and southern states. The times when we weren't in labor camps would find us in areas considered 'across the tracks' or 'in the bottoms'. These surroundings were never lacking in colorful characters or situations.

Anyway, I couldn't remember a time that I hadn't worked either in the fields with Momma or on my own. I was fortunate enough to begin some office work. I gained enough knowledge to get by on. Then, I honed and increased my office and interviewing skills. I found this to be viable and valuable to not having to do the manual labor type jobs anymore. I got to meet some of the most interesting people. The men were of a whole other breed but after pretty much the same thing. I met and worked with the demon possessed, deranged, high school drop outs to the proud, arrogant Ph.D.'s.

I was almost beginning to hate all men but not quite. I just hated the lies, the deceit, and the whoredom. It got to where I barely saw my kids. When I did see them, I was either too tired or too involved in my own issues to enjoy them.

Who is this Jesus?

In all of that, I had never come to know Jesus Christ as Savior and Lord. I had been baptized I don't know how many times, but I never knew Him. It took someone who was going through some turmoil of her own to introduce me to this Jesus. She was by no means perfect, but it was obvious she was in love and at peace.

This woman loved Jesus. She had something I wanted and I listened when she talked about Him. In the midst of her pain, she took the time to reach out to me. I guess she saw what a mess I was and allowed compassion to override her personal pain.

She invited me to her church. Though it seemed somewhat primitive, I met God in that place! There was a lot of passion, excitement, crying and pleading. A lot of emotion but not a whole lot of basic teaching to assure a solid foundation. I made many, many mistakes while there. I was in error so many times I felt like the word 'idiot' should be plastered on my forehead.

However, I started there and I'll never be able to thank them enough. I learned something there that has stayed with me ever since: commitment. That little group of people knew what it was to be committed in the face of adversity and opposition. That was the beginning of my walk with God.

What I learned there has helped sustain me and kept me from losing my mind over the years.

Breaking Away and the Mission

My friend and I eventually broke away from that congregation. We ended up starting a small mission-type church. I believed I was being led by God. Only He knows whether it was His leading or our own restlessness.

At first, I was considered the leader, the founder, the visionary for that small band of old school type individuals. Even the thought of it scares me now. I don't know why I was the leader. I didn't see any special abilities within myself that were more than anyone else had. Nevertheless, we were faithful as we understood the word. For a time, we met at each other's homes. Eventually, we rented a small, inexpensive, run down building for services. From that base, we did street services, door-to-door visitations, prayer meetings, shut-ins, other outreach activities as we felt appropriate.

Yes, we were a small group of Believers but we believed in what we were doing. Who we represented! That's more than I can say for a great number of folk today. Anyway, we each lived in our own corners of perceived hells here on earth. Mine was multifaceted.

This is just a little piece of the pie, a tiny little bit of God's grace toward me.

Please hear me: I do not brag or boast about any of this. I gratefully bow in submission as I acknowledge Jesus and His faithfulness toward me. He has always been faithful even when I was faithless and went a whoring after other gods; He still cared about me and loved me. He still took care of me. I am so reminded of the love story of the love story portrayed by Hosea and Gomer. That's what I see when I look at God's love for me.

All of this took place during husband #2 phase. All of his flaws were still very much in place. I was in error up to my neck and didn't even know it. The one thing that endeared me to him was what I saw as his genuine love for my girls. He was the biological father to the youngest. Lord knows he had some issues but he had me thoroughly convinced that he loved them all – equally! I knew he loved them all differently but I honestly thought the love was equally and appropriately distributed as a father. Oh, the tangled web we weave when we so desperately want to believe. If only I had paid attention. If only I hadn't been so selfishly wrapped up in myself. There is much more to this than I can address right now. Maybe we'll do a book on this all by itself. We already have enough material.

You know, he and I would probably still be together had it not been for these next events I'm about to describe to you. Remember I told you that he had a weakness for marijuana and women, right? Well, sometimes the women – his women – would get the urge to call the house. Somehow, I believe he had them convinced that I would not give him a divorce. I let each one of them know (when we spoke by phone and sometimes in person) that he could have a divorce at any time he so desired. I went on to explain that he was free to leave and that I had invited him to do so on many occasions. I don't think they believed me because he was so convincing. I know. He made me feel like a complete idiot frequently.

One young woman called while he was out and we just chatted. She let me know that she was in the hospital in a town a few hours south of us. I asked what she needed. She said she was calling because she wanted him (my husband) to know that she had miscarried his baby.

I'll be perfectly honest with you. This guy was and probably still is a very likeable man. I mean if you needed a friend, he would be the one to choose! I have actually seen him take the blame for things I knew he wasn't guilty of just to protect his friends. He took the blame on himself to keep them from getting into trouble. *Imagine that!* He just wasn't good husband material.

Not One but Two Babies!

Then came the last straw. Mind you now, I was still the leader of this church. I was preaching, teaching, witnessing, evangelizing, praying, laying on hands, casting out demons (I didn't personally do much of this one). I was doing all the stuff you're _supposed_ to do as an upstanding, righteous woman of God (as was my understanding at the time). After the death of my last remaining maternal aunt, I began to slack off from church.

There was this guy who was what we called a 'shade-tree mechanic'. This means he probably wasn't certified or insured, didn't have a shop, you got no guarantees and a lot of his work was actually done under a shade tree in his or someone else's yard. Anyway, I used to get him to work on my cars from time to time. He was pretty good and would work with me allowing me to pay him by installments if I didn't have all of the money. I didn't know much else about him and quite frankly, never had an interest.

Well, he just happened to be available during one of my moments of weakness after one of husband #2's escapades. He asked me out. I went. He said a bunch of stuff I wanted to hear. I listened. I said 'yes'. Oh, boy was that ever a serious mistake. I still have trouble believing I fell for it so easily! But I did. _SUCKER! SET UP! SILLY WOMAN!_ II Timothy 3:6-7

The problem was pretty simple. I had been putting up a façade of such strength and bravery for a very long time. I had nothing, no power behind the façade because I never bothered to seek out the Living Truth. I didn't have a deep relationship with Christ. I had a shallow, surface, thin-ice type of relationship. I kept up the front for as long as I could. I had been doing this for so long that when the tough stuff came, it couldn't hold up under pressure. It broke down. I broke down. My love for Jesus was real. My salvation was real but my foundation was weak and lacking and that was my fault. Expectations of myself, my faith, and my demands on co-laborers in Christ were unrealistlc, In error. The only thing I really had was the love of Jesus. That was real and it lasted through everything I went through. That is the Only Thing that kept me from completely losing my mind! I kid you not! I thank God for His Grace, His Mercy, and His Love!

You see, while still living with husband #2, God had literally shown me in a dream that he, my husband had a baby with another woman. Yes, this had taken place during the time we were living together as husband and wife. Naturally, when I approached him about it, he claimed total innocence. He said he was, once again, just a victim of my suspicious mind. He said he had no outside children. If there were any problems with us they were all in my head. (Trust issues). I swallowed that one until the day the process server showed up at the front door of our home.

The papers were for him but as usual, he wasn't there. This was a female process server and I could tell she really didn't want to give me the paperwork. I just thought it was something about the kids he had before we got married. The lady had actually gone back to her vehicle without giving me the papers. Then, I suppose she realized she had to do her job. She came back, verified he did live there and that I was his wife. I assured her that he did and I was. She handed me the papers after I signed for them. Then she quickly left after apologizing. Now I'm confused. So I began reading the court summons. Thank God the girls were at school and I was at home alone!

As I began reading the summons, I felt as if the breath, my very life had been knocked out of me. It was similar to having a football player running full force and hitting you in the stomach. Another way I thought of it was like falling from a really high tree branch, landing flat on your stomach and face. I couldn't breathe for what seemed like minutes but I'm sure it was only seconds. Not only was there one baby, but according to the summons there were now two children he had fathered – both younger than all of my girls.

For a while, I just sat on the floor, screaming, rocking back and forth and hugging myself. I think I lost all sense of reality at this point. Then I began looking everywhere for clues, hints, evidence of his shenanigans and unfaithfulness. I found paperwork in our truck showing he had put the children in his name on our last wedding anniversary! That's when I really lost it, went berserk, totally but temporarily insane, nuts, crazy, out of my tree.

This was 1985. We had been together since 1973. It felt as if the walls of our bedroom had been made of glass and everyone knew it but me.

I felt like he had said to the world that he wasn't satisfied with me even though he wouldn't leave. That he could have two or even three families if he wanted to. I was the only one in the dark. I found out much later that he had taken the girls, my girls, by to see his outside children. I felt so used, betrayed, foolish, useless, like nothing.

I went looking for him with murder in my heart. If it had not been for God's intervention, I believe I would have killed him. I went riding up and down the streets of our small town determined to hunt him down like the dog I thought he was and kill him!

I found the house of another woman he was seeing and knocked on the door. The landlord came out and talked to me. He said, "Miss, I don't know you but I know you don't belong out here like this. Don't make yourself look bad. Don't do this to yourself. Why don't you just go on home? If he's any kind of a man, he'll come home after this."

Well, I listened to him and left in the truck. Naturally, he (husband #2) had not come to the door and the woman inside said he wasn't there. What else was she supposed to say? 'Your husband is here but he's not coming out right now?' Probably wouldn't have been a good thing to say to me right then.

As I got a little ways down the road, I saw him walking on the side of the street. He was behaving as if he didn't have a clue about what was going on. At first, I tried to run over him. Then he jumped onto the running board of the passenger side of the truck. I stuck the gun in his face and pulled the trigger. (Oh, yeah I had one!) Now, goodness and mercy caught up with me. The gun snapped or jammed or whatever they do when they don't work.

The look on his face was almost enough to satisfy me but not quite. I was in so much pain. I felt a rage, hatred, a range of emotions seemingly all at once. Those emotions had overtaken me and I wanted him dead. Then I realized I could have killed him. I began to shake violently. I don't know where he went but I thank God that the gun didn't discharge. I checked it out later and it still had bullets in it. I shot it just to be sure it did work. It worked fine. That was the Divine intervention of God. No doubt in my mind.

A Silly Woman and a Shade Tree Mechanic

Needless to say, thank God, I didn't kill him but I did the next worst thing. I hooked up with the shade tree mechanic. I cast caution, good sense, common sense, reputation and God to the wind. I moved out of my home into his home. Against the advice and counsel of family and the few friends I had left, I married him when my divorce became final.

He was husband #3. Although I had seen a little of his unpredictable behavior before we got married, I chalked it up to his high strung personality, the stress we had both been under. Anything except the truth.

You see, I ignored some things that were key elements, important elements. Indicators of what life with him would be like. He never seemed to have a balance in his emotions. I mean never. He was either extremely nice – you know the sickly, sticky sweet kind – or he was extremely cold and unresponsive. He would punch a wall, throw a dish, bang his fist on a table, his driving was erratic, fast and dangerous. Everything was extreme. I ignored it or made excuses for it. He was a man out of control.

Up until the day we got my divorce papers for husband 2 and married each other, I had this uneasy, gnawing feeling in the middle of my stomach. I had even been warned by a woman of God, a woman of integrity. She had been troubled by God and instructed to tell me that if I married him, he would make my life miserable. He would try to destroy me and my loved ones. He would definitely try to destroy and kill me. I didn't listen. I married him anyway. My youngest daughter once asked me what it was that caused me to marry him. I told her that I felt obligated. She said: "What a reason to get married." Truer words were never spoken. The reason: embarrassment, obligation, fear, foolishness and feeling trapped. The consequences: danger, devastation, death of my babies' innocence, not knowing what else to do, anguish, pain and mental unbalance.

Honestly, I was so embarrassed. So ashamed. So clueless as to what I should do. I had made such a mess of things - everything! Not only had I done it to myself, I had embarrassed the church, my family, my children, and my friends. What else could I do? I had to make it right, didn't I? I had embarrassed God. I had let them all down. I couldn't face people until I made this thing right. And the only way to make it right was to marry him. After all, he had been good to me and the girls, hadn't he? I felt obligated. I owed it to him. I had sinned and thought the only way I (notice the _"I"_ there) could remove the blemish was to marry this man. Once again, what a tangled web we weave...... I owed him nothing! Nothing! But, I didn't know that, at least not at the time.

So, we got married. Less than one month after the marriage ceremony, he beat and abused me within moments of what I knew was the end of my life. Afterwards, naturally, he apologized profusely. He said: I made him crazy, he loved me, I made him do it. I got the typical treatment which included flowers, phone calls and all of the niceties of the 'honeymoon stage'. That was the beginning of many more horrific, terrifying incidents. From that day throughout our sick relationship, I got his fist in my face, my face in the dashboard, and his foot in my side. This scarred and scared me, my girls, and other family members. He never hit one of the girls but I can't tell you the damage witnessing that kind of violence did to them. They didn't see it often but how often does it take to do harm? I broke up with him several times before the final one. They still saw far too much violence, they also saw their mother in a situation no child should ever see and no person should ever be in.

I heard someone say once that: "Pain plants the flag of reality in the fortress of a rebel heart". God any red flags flying in your life?

The Demon Came Out

Two incidents, really three, come to mind that I let happen and they still haunt me.

#1:   I was driving away in my car, leaving him and he was determined that I wouldn't. At least not alive. He chased me and the two younger girls in his car. We were just trying to get away. I wanted to avoid another confrontation but he became so angry. His face was like a grotesque mask of sheer rage. I don't know if I've ever seen a demon but if I were to try and describe one to you, it would have been his face and demeanor. His intent was obvious that day. He tried to run me off the road. He planned on killing me and I knew it. He blocked the road with his car and then tried to burst my windows to open the door. I floored it and he held onto my side mirror. He finally had to let go and we got away.

#2:   He literally ripped my clothes off of me in a fit of anger. He beat me in front of the girls and two of his sons. The only things I had on when he finished were my bra and panties. He cursed me as if I were a thieving, mongrel dog. He kicked me in my sides and any other place he could find to put his foot. My babies were so scared. God help me and any other woman who has been through this. Help the ones going through it right now! Does any of this sound familiar to you? The really sad part about this is, I can remember seeing this same kind of thing when it happened to my mother.

#3:   We were outside arguing. This time it was a standoff. He had the shovel and I had the machete. Every time he cursed me, I cursed him back.

We got so loud; I'm really surprised the police weren't called. I was ready to commit murder and I think he knew it. He left me alone ….. At least for a while.

God's Faithfulness to Me

There were many other times of humiliation, degradation, and harm.....
BUT GOD! I kid you not, throughout the whole five years of that crazy,
tumultuous relationship; God was still taking care of me. He was still faithful. He
preserved my life. He protected me. You and I both know that I didn't deserve it
but He still gave it. I have scars, physical, mental, and emotional... but GOD
delivered me from the hands of the enemy. He (the man) was not the **THE**
enemy. He just worked for him.

Satan is my enemy. *The enemy*. I had walked away from the safety of
my Savior's arms right into satan's territory when I became disobedient to God.
I played right into satan's hands. I was the guilty one who cooperated with his
plan, walked away from God. I was in disobedience and WE paid dearly for it.
Remember in the Old Testament where God actually used the enemies of the
Israelites to bring them back to Him? God can use whatever and whomever He
wants to in order to turn our hearts back to Him.

According to scripture, I had every right to leave and divorce husband
#2. He was an adulterer and practiced it on a regular basis without repentance.
Leaving him was not my sin. The adulterous relationship with another man was
my sin. I moved into the house with him and took my babies with me. Taking
them into that atmosphere, an environment of violence and confusion, away
from God – that was my sin. He was an unbeliever and I took us into that hell
hole he called home. This was all before the divorce. Father of Mercy, help us
foolish, emotionally controlled women to wake up! It's not worth it. A few

minutes of sensual pleasure and a few lies to soothe our sin craved soul is not worth the years of devastation and poison. It just isn't worth it.

Before I finally left him for the last time, he was blackmailing me. He had already ruined all four tires on my car, called my job, harassed me, and threatened to do more. Now mind you, he had begun to step out and enjoy some outside treats with other women. He was just still determined to control and handle me. Why did I put up with it? What did he hold over my head?

He and I had committed a crime together. Yeah, when you start sinking – I don't care how smart you think you are – there is no limit to what you'll do. He told me that if I didn't keep up at least a portion of our sick relationship, he would turn state's evidence and I would go to jail. He kept pointing out how bad it would be for my girls if I wasn't around. For a long time, I was convinced and went along with him just to stay out of jail. As long as I let him come over from time to time or I went to him, he kept quiet. However, he never let me forget that he would do what he said. You see, the authorities didn't have enough evidence to prosecute without his testimony.

Eventually, I'd just had enough and refused to see him anymore. I was trying to get my life and the girls' lives back together. I was going to a good church. The fellowship was good. The teaching was very good and I was finally building a good foundation in the Word. For the first time in a very long time, I was, at last, looking forward to waking up in the mornings. Anyway, I stopped seeing him and true to his word, he turned state's evidence. I was arrested on my job. He was protected. What if I had turned State's evidence first?

Suicide or Sympathy?

You would think I'd had enough, wouldn't you? NOT! You see, part of my behavior pattern, my sickness, was co-dependency. When I found myself without a job, alone and hurting a lot, not sure about so many things including whether I could survive life in prison or not, what would happen to my babies, I reverted to my old habit of clinging. I traipsed right back to him. This was more than a relapse. Folk, this was insanity. The night I went back to him, I found his new girlfriend and her children there. I discovered that they were now frequent visitors, overnighters, in our mobile home (the one I bought and paid for).

That should have been it for me but it wasn't. My husband, his lover, and her children stayed in the living room that awful night. I stayed in the bedroom, alone. I turned on a local Christian television program and commenced to humiliating myself. I was determined to make him take me back. After all, I was alone. I had made the newspaper headlines and the evening news. I didn't have a job. I couldn't take care of my girls. Where else could I go? I was ruined and headed for jail. I needed him (I thought). What he had been saying all along was true. Nobody wanted me and I was alone. *(Battle of the mind!)*

With all of these thoughts in my head, I couldn't concentrate on the television program. I sank deeper and deeper into depression while my husband lay sleeping in the next room with another woman. I found some pills in our bathroom and swallowed them. I don't even remember what they were. They weren't working fast enough, although I did start to feel faint and somewhat numb. I found razor blades in the cabinet and totally gave up. I began to cut myself. I slashed my wrist, my arm, the backs of my legs and ankles until I could see white cartilage. I watched the whole gory mess as if it wasn't really me. I was there but detached. I was a mad woman as I cut deeper and deeper, actually seeing the inside workings in shades of pink, red, and white. At one point, there was so much blood that I nearly passed out. I was in the bathtub. He found me and called 911.

Needless to say, I ended up Baker Acted in the mental ward of the hospital due to the suicide attempt. Did I want to commit suicide or did I want his sympathy? I wanted to stop the hurting and thought sympathy from him would do it.

I won his heart again (whatever that was worth) but the next eleven months were indescribable. It was as if hell had unleashed its fury just for me. The stories I could tell you about the mental ward of that hospital were nothing compared to what it was like living with him again. What was I thinking? That's just it. I wasn't thinking very much and not clearly at all. I was just *f-e-e-l-i-n-g*. Letting my emotions rule and control me.

This was the same problem I had seen modeled before me. She had seen it modeled before her. We had all seen some form of this same sick thing. I had more or less 'caught' the behavior (even though I had sworn I would not do this!), I did it anyway! I had stuffed a lot of emotions, fears, anger, insecurities, and hurt and failed to deal with it. Ignoring the problem does not make it go away.

What About My Babies?

Now that he and I were back together, can you imagine what my daughters must have felt like?? Totally confused. I once heard it said that it is better for children when their mother dies than when she loses her mind. What about when she abandons them? *What about my babies?*

I made feeble, lame, and sad attempts to get them settled with folk they could stay with while I was in jail. I was sure that I would be spending 15 – 25 years in prison. Only one of my girls was in a satisfactory place. My oldest was with Momma and then on her own. My middle one was with her father (he was separated from his wife) but that arrangement didn't work out. Then she was with a girlfriend of hers but that didn't work out either. Eventually, she went to live with the oldest (who by this time had a little boy of her own). My baby girl ended up living with a couple from church (thank God). They had all tried living with Momma for a while but it just didn't work.

They needed me. They needed their mother in her right mind. I can only say that in those 11 months, I was a very irresponsible, selfish, and foolish parent.

I was going to court anywhere from 1-2 times a month expecting them to lead me off in handcuffs each time. I thought if I could at least get the girls settled in somewhere, I could have some semblance of peace while doing my jail time. I knew for a certainty that I could not bring them back into that situation of violence but I wasn't strong enough to stay out myself.

Why did I go back to him? To make a last ditch effort at a marriage that never should have taken place? To feel that I really could succeed at marriage, even if only for a little while? Foolishness? To gain his trust and loyalty then leave him to go off to prison? I don't know. I do know that it was part of the sickness. I saw the same thing when I worked in Social Services. Day in and day out, mothers abandoning children almost as frequently as men used to. Some of them to follow some sad excuse of a man. Others just felt they had to get away.

I do know it was a seriously bad call and it still hurts when I think of the pain I caused my children. I suppose I could plead temporary insanity. What else could it be? What else could cause a mother to abandon her daughters? Ugly word, isn't it? Abandon. Anyway, through it all, I kept waiting to hear the judge hand down the sentence as to how many years I would have to serve for the crime I committed.

Week after week, he (my husband) would forbid me sending any money to the girls. I always found a way. I could have very limited contact with them by phone. I was occasionally allowed to attend church but I couldn't put on make-up or look nice. He monitored phone calls and mail. I was on the clock from the time I left the house until I returned. I was a nervous as a cat in a house full of hungry bulldogs by the time I got back.

When I think about it now, I realize I was already in prison. He was the warden and as long as I followed his rules, things were tolerable. When I broke a rule, I got solitary confinement or some other type of punishment. Some of the things I say here are very mild compared to other things that actually took place Trust me, folk. God is a good God.

Now get this. For a little while, before he turned State's evidence, I had an affair. Yep! Believe it or not. As scared as I was of him. As fearful and co-dependent as I was, I actually stepped out on him! That was my way of saying (without really saying it out loud to him): *"No matter what you do to me, you don't know everything. You don't really own me! You can't dominate every part of me. You only have partial control. You don't even know me!"*

The human spirit was never meant to be dominated. I tell you this just to let you know that even though he thought he had me completely under his control, under his power, a part of me still rebelled. It was sin. No doubt about it, but just think about that for a minute. He was so sure that he had me under his thumb, that he had me behaving like his remote controlled robot. Yet, I rebelled!

I knew that if he ever found out he would kill me. Yet, I dared to cross him and I rebelled! The human spirit is amazing. The affair wasn't even that great. I enjoyed the mystique, the danger, the fact that I had a secret. It seemed the only way I could continue getting out of my relationship with him. It was my way of keeping a smidgen of hope alive. I would get away.

I missed my girls something awful. I used the excuse of trying to get them settled somewhere before I went to prison. That's what I said to anyone who asked. I told them, him and myself that. Even if that was part of the reason, it was still just selfishness. It was part of a learned pattern. It was a generational thing. I was controlled by my emotions and had selfishly abandoned my babies. For what? A bankrupt marriage, a defunct relationship, an impossible situation. A man who never meant me any good at all. Sad, isn't it?

Now I was afraid that if they were there with me, he might cross the line and hurt them, too. He wasn't above threatening me with doing them harm in order to control me. Besides, I didn't want them to see him beat me anymore. I also knew there was a distinct possibility of my ending up dead or of me even killing him. So why didn't I just leave? Your guess is about as good as mine but some things still baffle me. I do believe that God supernaturally intervened to keep them from what was happening to me and my sick co-dependency issues as well as from him and his violent tendencies.

There are no words to tell you about or describe the shame and guilt I have had to face and deal with over the years. Again, all I can say is BUT GOD!

Day in and day out as I headed for a temporary job I'd found, I would just scream at the top of my lungs and ask God to help me because I was a miserable, unhappy person. I needed to be with my babies but I was convinced that each month would be my last on the outside.

After all the months of court rooms, lawyers, continuances, public defenders, legal jargon and pleadings, it was finally time for sentencing. It was time to take another deep breath and bite the bullet. I was about to get what I deserved.

A Broken Spirit? - *BUT GOD!*

May of 1990. He (my husband) went with me to the sentencing. To this day, I can tell you that I expected no less than a 15 year sentence to be handed down. I was resigned to what I knew I deserved. AGAIN, I SAY ***BUT GOD!*** If ever I have seen the divine intervention of Almighty God, I saw it that day. I was a recipient of it and I'll never forget it. I was a direct recipient of God's Grace and nobody, I repeat: ***NOBODY*** had to tell me!

The prosecutor told the judge that jail time would break my spirit! That's right! The one who was there to make sure I went to jail said that. The one who was there to fight for justice, to be sure the law was adhered to, spoke on my behalf! Have you ever heard of anything like that in your life? I haven't. My public defender had advised me to plead guilty (because I was) so I did. The judge looked like he wanted to take me home to his wife for them to care for me. He wanted to give me 3 years probation but the minimum that the law allowed was 5 years. So, I walked out of that courtroom with 5 years of probation, ordered to pay restitution and cost of supervision as opposed to the 15 years I expected.

Now, you tell me, what does the 'System' care about a broken spirit? What do the legal eagles care about what happens to an offender? That was Almighty God. Do you hear me? That was Almighty God pleading my case! God is able to change the hearts and minds of kings and rulers and He did!

Okay. Walking out of the courtroom, I felt like I was in a cloud or a fog of some kid. I couldn't believe it. I was actually walking out – unshackled! Then, my husband said (as we approached the car): "Now, we can bring the girls back home." Immediately, my thought was: "I can't do that to them. I can't bring them back into this." At that point, I kid you not, I heard what I was positive (and still am) was an audible voice that said: *"If you can't do it to them, then why would you do it to yourself?"* The voice was so clear and so loud that I looked over at my husband to see if he had heard it, too. He didn't have a clue. He was still talking about plans to bring this family back together. Totally clueless, folk!

Then I knew it was just for me and it was directly from God. It was at that moment that I knew what I had to do. God literally formed a plan in my mind. He laid out the entire plan of escape for me in a moment's time. He told me how to get away, when to get away, who I should go to and who should be involved in the whole process.

I've heard "The Word" before. I've had prophetic words before. I've experienced reading the Word and seeing a specific and yet different application stand out for me. But I had never had anything so clearly, unmistakably and directly from God before. So, I followed the plan God gave to me to the letter. I got away, finally for the very last time.

Somehow, I knew this was really it. My pain was still very real. It was like a tearing away from something you've grown very accustomed to. Even though it was deadly, like cancer, it was a hard thing to leave. Strange but at the same time, it felt good to go. I liken it to driving carelessly for years, speeding, ignoring the speed limits then having a major accident with the car totaled. Then looking back at the wreck as you walk away from it amazed that you could even stand up, let alone walk! Notice, I said a major wreck. That means something other than yourself was involved: a tree, a post, a guard rail, a cliff, maybe even an animal or two or perhaps, even other people. Damaged and broken, I walked away from that wreck and I've never been the same.

I had to start over again in everything. My confidence had been totally shattered. Career, finances, home, relationships with my kids, family, friends, church, and self-esteem – everything had to begin again. It was difficult. It was hard. It was a tough lesson but one good thing came out of it all: I have never again been tempted to leave or cut off fellowship with Jesus. NEVER! I have thought of many things but never of leaving Him. Through it all, God has been more than faithful. He has been very gracious.

So as the writers have penned these scriptures, I give you a spattering of my testimony: It is good for me that I have been afflicted, But now Lord, what do I look for? My hope is in You. Save me from all my transgressions: Do not make me the scorn of fools.; He lifted me out of the slimy pit, out of the mud and mire, He set my feet on a rock and gave me a firm place to stand. He put a new song in my mouth, a hymn of praise to our God. Many will see and fear and put their trust in the Lord; and we know that in all things God works for the good of those who love Him, who have been called according to His purpose.

There was another thing that came out of it. I had been considered manic depressive (or in today's terms, bi-polar) with suicidal tendencies for at least 25 years. God used that time to totally deliver me from the suicidal tendencies. He also taught me how to fight off (successfully) the temptation to succumb to depression. Miraculously, God healed and delivered me from that disease! Hallelujah! Hail to the King!

There was great damage but there has also been a great healing. Our family has suffered much devastation, much pain, much hurt ....BUT GOD!

I remember Him (GOD) telling me something during that time. I was starting a new career (from the bottom up), trying to find a place to live, get a car, and keep my head on straight all at the same time. I was experiencing such feelings of inadequacy and defeat. He promised me that He would take care of me and my girls. He did not promise that there would be no pain. Nor did He promise that there would be an easy road to recovery for us. But He did promise that He would take care of us.

Since all of the drama I have described took place, my girls have grown into beautiful young women. They each have their own families and are dealing with their own specific set of situations, circumstances and life. I'm here to help.

The Apology for All Men

There was a lot of healing that needed to take place inside of me and God has orchestrated it all. I devoured mounds of self-help books and the Bible as if my very life depended on it because it did. I found material on healing, relationships, soul ties, forgiveness, emotional and mental recovery, healthy friendships, co-dependency, love, marriage, singleness, wholeness, generational curses, blessings, holiness, time with God, praise, worship, and anything God would lead me to for my recovery.

I attended workshops, seminars, conferences, prayer groups, and counseling sessions. I was in church just about every time the door opened. I spent time with my Abba Father and He loved me to health. He let me crawl up on His lap, lay my head on His chest and He hugged me, cooed over me, sang to me, rocked me to sleep many a night. I had finally found peace in His arms. He personally guided me and directed me as to what I should do, where to go and get what I needed and I did. How I relish time alone with my Abba Father My personal relationship grew like a wild fire.

God used my Pastor a lot during that time to be a vessel of messages that I really needed to hear I didn't always agree with or even like some of the things but I needed all of it and I have learned to always agree with God. One time in particular stands out in my mind. We were in prayer and he (Pastor Filmore) came over to me and looked directly into my face and said: "I apologize to you for any hurt I have caused you and furthermore, I APOLOGIZE FOR EVERY MAN WHO HAS HARMED YOU IN THE PAST."

I can't tell you what that did for me. It was as if he had literally read my mind. He didn't have to do that. He could have dismissed the thought because he really hadn't done anything to me. But when he said that, I felt a breaking inside my inner man. The deepest part of me was touched and healed. Every fiber of my very being was touched. My heart felt as if it was melting into liquid love for Jesus at that point. Just imagine God using this man to catapult my inner healing, my total forgiveness for every man who had ever hurt me in my whole life, beginning with my earthly father.

I mention my earthly father because I felt he had abandoned me. I believed his abandonment; the absence of a father was responsible for a great part of what I had experienced.

Can you imagine the walls that were torn down? The ice that had formed around my heart to protect me was no longer needed. The methods I had in place to keep from being hurt again were no longer needed. God had assured me, in a moment of time, in an instant, that He would take care of me. As long as I was surrendered to Him, He would do it. He would cover me. I'll never forget that day. I don't know if Pastor realized the significance of it, but it changed my life. I began to learn how to really lavish love on The Savior. The kind of love that I had tried to lavish on men all of my life, I began to give it to Jesus and He received it! I'm talking about a rush beyond compare, a life changing event, The Love of a Lifetime, My Ultimate Love.

The Future Hope

That breaking was absolutely necessary. I wasn't mad with men anymore. I can honestly say I wasn't angry, excessively hurt or bitter. I wasn't even ticked off anymore. I just wasn't interested in a romantic love of any kind – no more Eros for me! I was content. I no longer craved a male/female relationship. I was totally content to be single and love on Jesus for the rest of my life. I didn't begrudge other women having men in their lives. I didn't talk down to them for wanting to be married or wanting companionship. I thought it was a noble and honorable thing. I had just had enough. I wasn't mean about it.

God had delivered me and I was happy. I was divorced and learning wholeness. I wished others well who still had the interest. I was beginning to experience wholeness and holiness unto the Lord. I realized no ordinary man could complete me. I didn't need a man to complete what God had started. My God would finish what He had started in me.

I lived with a friend of mine for a while then I went to a shelter for women. After that, I kind of bounced around a little bit but I meant what I said. I was happy being a single woman. Even during the times when it looked like I might have to sleep in my car, I was okay with that because I knew it was temporary.

I was getting to know my baby girl better. She was the only one (of the girls) who was interested in being around me at the time and I understood. We were financially challenged but it was working out. We had to live with my mother for a little while. We stayed there until God literally challenged and corrected me in the area of my attitude. He said until I became grateful and thankful right where I was, I would not be moving to the place He had lined up for me. I quickly told my baby girl and we both made attitude adjustments. We began to regularly thank God for having a place to live, for bringing us back together, for His mercy toward me in the court system. We discovered all kinds of wonderful things to thank Him for.

Shortly after that, God opened up an affordable housing situation for us and I couldn't have asked for a better arrangement. In fact, when we moved in, we had almost no furniture. The little we did have was transported in cars, but we moved in grateful.

Now the situation with the furniture was soon remedied by my good friend and my Pastor's wife, Carroll. I thank God for that woman. I really think she's gifted and besides that, she has a really big heart for people. Anyway, this woman found and purchased an entire living room set for me at a garage sale for $25! And it was a nice set. No junk. I told you she was gifted, didn't I? Then she had it delivered to us. Over the years, that set finally left my house and ended up in Tallahassee at school with my daughter.

I also remember Carroll and Pastor bringing over some twin beds for us. Just watching the two of them working together was an inspiration for me. I had never seen a healthy couple working together in harmony with each other. All they were doing was putting together bed frames but you could tell they had done this many times before – together. They worked like a well-oiled machine. As one. Simple everyday things become important life lessons when people are willing to share their lives. People willing to invest in the lives of others. Pouring themselves out. Being real friends. Giving of themselves. Vital...

Expect the Unexpected

Okay. So now I'm all set up in an apartment. Out on probation. I have a decent job and a car that works most of the time. My baby girl and I are learning to live in an attitude of gratitude. Church is going well. My relationship with Jesus is better than it has ever been. We're struggling financially but we're making it. What more could you ask for?

Out of the blue, along comes this single guy who loved Jesus as much as I did. I really didn't pay him much attention at first. He was just another fella – a brother in Christ. I was an uninterested, satisfied, single woman. I treated him with respect, cared about is growth in Christ, but that was it and I am so serious. I had no use for dating nor the concept of dating or any kind of close relationship at all! I am so for real on this. Then suddenly, things began to happen and we were literally thrown together – in ministry!

I was the Praise & Worship Leader. When he came to our church, he was a reluctant musician but we needed him and Pastor recruited him. It was all so very innocent. I think that God set it up. This brother started giving me 'the look'. You know, the one that can scare you or draw you. I started trying to find ways for us to never be alone because now I'm really scared! He let me know he had an interest in me and then I was confused and I told God. I actually fussed at God because I was so content. I didn't want anything to mess that up.

However, I began to notice his gentle manner and his genuine love for Jesus, his respect for women, and his honesty. Not at all like anything I'd ever experienced before. Note: all of this took place while we were both _busy doing church or church related work_.

Eventually, we went to God separately and then together, admitted our mutual attraction for each other and were soon married. Jeremiah 29:11 says: "For I know the thoughts that I think toward you, saith the Lord, thoughts of peace, and not of evil, to give you an expected end." I had one plan but my Abba Father had another. I should have known to expect the unexpected from Him by now, right?

Paul, my husband, is absolutely the kindest, most loving, considerate, loyal, affectionate and God-fearing man I have ever known. I said earlier that I believe God set us up. I believe He hand-picked and prepared Paul for me. Don't misunderstand me, we have had our struggles. From day one we've been challenged. I'm sure he's had his doubts just as I have during the times of transition and hard places. There was a lot of healing left to be done on both sides. Bottom line is that I know he loves God and finally, I know that he loves me. We've had to work through a lot of stuff because we both had our own baggage. We have cultivated a really great relationship over time. We genuinely love, respect, honor and value each other. In this marriage, there is no abuse! Glory to the Lamb of God!

For most of our married life, I worked in the social service sector. I've been home now (2003) for nearly 2 years. For almost a year of that time, we were caretakers for 5 of our 11 grandchildren. Now, I write, listen, pray and wait.

I do a monthly publication called 'S.W.I.M.' That's an acronym for Single Women In Ministry. This goes beyond the word single as in unmarried. It speaks to wholeness, being complete in Christ alone.

Paul and I conduct conferences by the same name geared toward healing the Body of Christ. We teach the Word and share our experiences, our struggles, defeats, failures, concerns and successes. God has instructed us to be open and honest about our lives, to bare our souls because of the nature of the ministry. This isn't always easy to do because, quite frankly, some of the stuff is downright embarrassing. The reason we do it is because we are directed, guided and encouraged by God. Our mission is to assist in reconciling; guiding people into deliverance and setting the captives free (Isaiah 61).

You see, just as my ex-husband would not have been able to blackmail me if I had told the truth myself, Satan cannot use his blackmail tactics on you if you tell it yourself. Confession. Then begin to walk in the freedom that God gives as only He can give. St. John 8:32 "Then you will know the truth, and the truth will set you free". Jesus is The Truth.

No Brag, Just Fact

Nothing I have written in this book was for my glory. Nothing was meant to sensationalize or promote me. Nothing was meant to disrespect or do harm to anyone. Everything was and is to show the sovereignty of Almighty God in the lives of His People. Yes, even those who are wayward but have a heart toward God. I'm to expose the plot of satan if you will open your eyes, open your ears and walk in the perfect plan God has for you.

Some things just don't seem fair. Some things may never be explained. All I know is: I am chosen, hand-picked, singled out for God's purpose. In Deuteronomy 7:6-9, I understand it to mean He did not choose us because of our number, our might, or our abilities. He is God, the Faithful God Who keeps covenant and He does what He wants, what He wills to do.

He knew that the things that I suffered and took my family through were the very things it would take to settle and establish me. He could have easily changed the course of my life at any time. He knew my makeup. He knew what I required in my stubborn insistence to be wayward, to stray, to nibble outside of the grazing area He outlined for me. He knew that I would continue to search until I realized that He really is the One for me and that He loved me unconditionally.

He also knew that if He told me to tell about my experiences, I would obey Him. He knew that I would love Him so much that the embarrassment would seem minimal compared to the healing that would take place in the lives of others.

Years ago, back in 1987-1988 He highlighted these scriptures for me. They are oftentimes what I go back to when I need to encourage myself. Ezekiel 47:1-12. Read it sometimes and see the parallel to my life as it was, how it is, and where God is taking me. I am convinced that the horrible pain I have shared as my experiences will continue to be used by God. Many of them already have been. Someday, another woman or a man will read this and be convicted by the Holy Spirit of God in order to turn around from the direction they're headed in. I pray that they will see my pain, my struggle, my victory and be convinced that God is fully able to deliver them from the hands of the enemy. If you're still breathing, it's not too late.

If there is still life left in your body, it is not too late. Have the courage to get out, go a different direction before it gets as bad as mine did. *Have the wisdom and gain some hope for the future when this book gets into your hands!*

God used countless numbers of people to get me out, encourage me once I got out, and counsel me when I began to doubt my ability to make it. They encouraged me to trust God and His strength, His ability to take me through. Some of my sisters and brothers in Christ at Freedom Ministries actually gave me bags of groceries, clothes, money. These were critical times for me because I had to be convinced that a woman with a felony on her record could make it. God used His people, my sisters and brothers, to encourage me. I know it was Him every step of the way.

Deuteronomy 32:1-4 was also for me. "Give ear, O Heavens, and I will speak; And hear, O Earth, the words of my mouth. Let my teaching drop as the rain, My speech distill as the dew, As raindrops on the tender herb, And showers on the grass. For I proclaim the name of the Lord: Ascribe greatness to our God. He is the Rock, his work is perfect; for all His ways are justice, A God of truth and without injustice; Righteous and Upright is He."

God knows that I am committed to tell how He rescued me. I will publish His mighty Name, the All Powerful, Kind, Merciful and Gracious God. I have promised and I will do it. As long as I have the gift, I will answer the call on my life to tell others of His goodness. I'll tell it. I pray that the Holy Spirit will spark, ignite, and increase faith in someone's heart and life. I pray you will be encouraged to give God free reign in your life

You know, I hear a lot of testimonies about people who have been abused. I believe every one of them especially when I hear some of the details. Part of what God has placed on my heart is that yes, the abuse took place and the abuser is guilty. The other part is my part in it and my choices that have hurt so many other people. I have had to face those things and acknowledge my responsibility and my wrong doing in all of it. Once I came to that place, as ugly, unattractive and painful as it was, that is when God began to do a specific work in me for witnessing to others.

This is not a pleasant thing that I do when I expose my failures. But if you've read the scriptures in Ezekiel 47, you'll know that this isn't just for me and mine. I do this perhaps for your daughter who ran away from home. Perhaps she feels she is obligated to do what her pimp or boyfriend tells her to do. Maybe she thinks she has to obey the demon possessed man she lives with. Maybe she doesn't know she has a choice. I do this for the little girl who has seen her momma get beat up night after night and thinks this is normal. I do this for that little girl who is looking for somebody to love her because daddy left home and she felt abandoned. I do this for the girl or boy who was molested once or raped repeatedly by a relative, a trusted family friend, an authority figure, a religious leader, etc.

I do this for you because you think this is the only way you can make it and you don't know any other way to make ends meet. I do this for you. Yes, you who have been convinced that sex is the only thing that works to get you what you want, even for a little while. For you who have been convinced that you're nothing but trash because that's what you've been told. You've been told you're stupid, ugly, fat, absolutely worth nothing, unattractive, dumb, lazy, and nasty, a loser, no good in bed or anywhere else, and damaged goods. He may have even told you that nobody else would have you and you're lucky he still takes up any time with you.

He may have said all of that, but if you'll take the time to read these scriptures, you'll find out what God says about you. Psalm 115:16; Psalm 126:1-6; Psalm 139:1-18; Isaiah 43:1-7; I Peter 1:1-9; I Peter 1:19-23; I Peter 2:1-9; II Peter 1:1-4; Deuteronomy 33:11; Psalm 127:2; Romans 8:28-38; I Samuel 26:9; Isaiah 62:1-12; St. John 3:16; Ephesians 1:4-8; 11-14; St. John 17:20-23. You are precious, highly favored and most valuable to God.

Precious in His Sight

You are precious, valuable, more than a conqueror, constantly thought of, prayed for, beautiful, loved, a jewel, a precious gem, and a precious stone. I tell you these things praying and trusting the God of my salvation will take you on a treasure hunt in His Word. If you do this, you'll discover for yourself the value God placed on you and still does.

Don't let anyone tell you that you're not worth anything. You are so highly thought of that God gave His Most Precious Lamb, His Dear Son, Jesus the Christ, as a Ransom for you. Did you know that? Jesus came to earth on a Rescue Mission, a Mission of Mercy. Not just anybody could handle this mission. We needed the Special Forces to take care of this. God came in the form of a Man on a Mission seeking you!

He came to this place to settle the matter started in the Garden of Eden when Adam gave up his authority and sinned. The penalty for sin is death. The sin debt had to be paid and God exacted that penalty on Jesus for 'whosoever will, let him come.' The secret is: we have to come. He doesn't force.

Jesus came willingly as the Perfect, Sinless Lamb, and the Perfect Sacrifice. He paid the debt, the penalty. The debt is now paid in full! The Only One qualified to pay for all times, for all people *did just that!* Anyone who wants their sin debt paid off can come to Jesus, Our Kinsman Redeemer – but you have to come. It isn't a given or an automatic thing. You have to come and accept Him and the whole package will then be yours. St. Mark 16:14-16; Romans 3:23; Romans 4:7-8; St. John 3:36; Romans 8:1-11; Romans 9:33; Romans 10:9-11; I John 1:5-10.

And that's just the beginning – when you learn how to and then choose to walk away from sin. The Ultimate Rush from The Ultimate Answer. Your Burden Bearer I Peter 1:7.

Jesus, My Redeemer, My Lord, My God, My King, My Healer, My Salvation. To Him, I give all Praise, All Glory, All Credit for what He has done. What very marvelous, wonderful things He has completed. He is Praiseworthy.

Keeping It Real

Was my faith shaken when I was in the middle of those self-made storms? Yes. In fact, even though I created and then walked into my own storms, for the most part, everything was shaken except God's unfailing, undying, unfathomable, deep and faithful love for me.

I just want to keep it real. I don't want you to think it will be all peaches and cream or roses without thorns. I want you to know there will be tough days and probably some sleepless nights but God will see you through.

He loved me through attempted suicides, failed marriages, adultery, fornication, theft, lies, deceit, hatred, murderous thoughts, intents and plans, unfaithfulness, anger, bitterness, rage, depression, cowardice, selfishness, ungratefulness, treachery, deviant behaviors and thoughts, rebellion and witchcraft, mental illness, disobedience, favoritism, prejudice, lack, pride and abandonment. He loved me through it all and I'm still here!

Do you think He could love you any less or any more? *NO!*

Do you think His hand is disabled?

Is His arm shortened?

Is His strength decreased?

Is His eyesight diminished?

Are His ears too far away to hear?

Do you not know? Have you not heard?

Job 42:1-2; Isaiah 40:21-23; Jeremiah 32:17.

Nothing is too hard for God.

Luke 1:37; Matthew 17:19-20.

And with God, nothing is impossible for you. I remember one of the times we (my Mom, my sister and I) were running away from my stepfather in the middle of the night. He was so drunk his words were slurred and he mixed some things up. He said: "My arm is sharp and my knife is strong." All of this just before he threw a tire rim through the kitchen window at Momma because she wouldn't let him in the house.

When I think about that kind of stuff, I'm only encouraged to remember the Word of God which lets me know: His Arm is Strong. His Word is sharper than a two-edged sword cutting asunder, dividing soul and spirit. He even designs us as iron sharpening iron for one another. God is not confused. He is not drunk or disoriented. He is not lacking in anything. He knew even back then when I was no more than 6 or 8 years old that I would survive the abuse, the family tree and generational curses, the rebellion, the catastrophic events. He knew and He walked with me through it all.

Chance or Choice?

So, wherever you are, if you want to change your location and the direction of your future, now is a really good time. You see, your destiny is not by chance or happenstance but by your choice. If I had a dime for every time I've heard: 'If only I had done this' or 'If only I hadn't done that', I would be a very wealthy woman. All you really have is right now. So with God on your side, you can. I'm a living witness. He can, He wants to, and He will help you, strengthen you, empower you, direct you, change you, and cover you.

Isaiah 41:10-13 "Fear not for I am with you; Be not dismayed, for I am your God. I will strengthen you, Yes, I will help you. I will uphold you with My Righteous right hand. Behold, all those who were incensed against you shall be ashamed and disgraced; They shall be as nothing. And those who strive with you shall perish. You shall seek them and not find them – those who contended with you. Those who war against you shall be as nothing, as a nonexistent thing. For I, the Lord, your God, will hold your right hand, saying to you, 'Fear not, I will help you.'" That does not mean you won't have obstacles. It means you will have help when there are obstacles.

There were things that happened in my family before I became an adult that affected, hurt and damaged me. I took on that guilt, that shame, that responsibility, those curses. I kept those things and they built up within the walls of my mind. I pondered them and tucked them away in my heart. I held onto them.

Then came additional things when I was a young girl, an adolescent, a teenager, a young woman. There were things so horrible, so indescribable that I continued to hold them while trying to figure out what to do with them. There was so much stuff that the walls of my heart were beginning to burst with pain and grief. My mind was equally troubled and I needed an outlet.

In a situation like that, who do you go to? Who can you tell? Who can you trust? At that time, I really didn't know. Just like some of you. The people you should be able to trust aren't trustworthy. The ones you have trusted failed. Where do you go? First and foremost, you go to God. You pour out your heart and get in His Word for instructions.

There are many reasons, I'm sure, but no valid excuses for abuse. Domestic violence had been part of my life for as long as I could remember. The little town where I spent most of my childhood to late teens was just full of it. The families there (including my own) had at least 1-2 episodes of violence weekly. We were considered the normal ones the families who didn't fight were considered middle or upper class in our neighborhood. In fact, some of us even called them 'uppity'.

We could sit on our porches or in our houses and know what was going on in just about any other house on the block. It was a very common thing to hear muffled thuds against the walls, glass windows breaking, tussles, scuffles or shrieks and cries for help. Furniture falling, sliding across the floor, bodies impacting each other, fists meeting faces or threats of a kitchen utensil being used as a weapon – all of this was commonplace. The children would often run outside and huddle together in fear for their mother's life. Sometimes believing their own lives might be in jeopardy. The usual time was on the weekend when the adults could let their hair down, so to speak, and relax. However, there was some weekday rough stuff, too. You know, that stuff was so imbedded in my mind that I can still hear some of the women; desperate, defeated women. Yes, times were tough. Things were hard and money was often tight but that should never be an excuse to do damage to anyone, especially the ones we're supposed to love and protect. It just shouldn't be.

The scenes are still clear, even vivid in my mind some forty years or so later. They'd be huddled on the floor, crumpled up in the fetal position in a corner. They made futile efforts to avoid their attacker's fist or foot. Always trying to protect their faces or even vital organs from an onslaught of physical blows. The verbal stuff was lethal. Some of them would say things in rapid shotgun or machine gun fire like: "Don't stop now, you so-and-so! Go ahead, *hit me!* That's right, you sorry, no good dog! You're a real man now. Yeah, *kick me!* Don't leave, yet. Is that all you've got? Why don't you *hit me again*? I know you're not finished. Just kill me. That the only thing left to do. Just kill me!"

These and many more statements like it would ring out in the night, from house to house. It was almost like a fever. You know, one house would get started and before long almost everyone had a fight going. It was like the fire got started in one house and ignited all the rest. I witnessed and heard this stuff from the time I was around 2 years old until I was at least 25. Some of it came from other people's houses but eventually, it began to come from my house. Hence comes the name of this book*: 'Hit Me, Kick Me, Hit Me Again'.*

I guess some of the women were tired. Others had given up hope long before we moved there. I suppose you can become accustomed to just about anything, accept anything, and become acclimated to anything. Lord God, I never got used to it and I'm so glad!

Some things that happened hurt so bad that ever so often, I took to running away from home. When that didn't really help (there are some horror stories on that subject, too), I would escape into books. I would read books that took me to faraway countries, other time periods, other places, make believe families and the 'ideal' lives of other people, fiction. I would lose myself in those books. The walls of my heart and my own life were so filled with pain and anguish that I tried to ignore them. Real life was just too tough so I tried to get away as often as I could. It worked for a while, but eventually, I had to come back to it.

That's what started it. I didn't know how to deal with my real world. I didn't know how to fight or stay afloat, so I tried to bring my fantasy world into the real word. I tried to make it become what I read about or dreamed about instead of seeing it for what it really was. Somehow, I began confusing the real world with my make believe world. I began to see those men (bad choices) as Knights on White Horses who had come to rescue me from the dungeon (my home life). There were no Knights or Prince Charmings in my neck of the woods, but in my dreams there were.

Follow the Instructions

Then, I finally realized that there was A Prince Who wanted to rescue me. The Prince of Peace, The King of Glory had me on His mind and in His plan all of the time. He had been there all along to protect me from even worse devastation and get me through the horrors of my childhood.

He had given me parents to protect and nurture me. It was not His fault that they failed in any area. Nor was it mine! It was theirs. They either by omission or commission missed the mark. They sinned. They did not live up to their part of the bargain.

Now, on that same note, it was not my children's fault that I failed them. It was not God's fault, either! Yeah, I can look at my past and my upbringing for some history but bottom line: I sinned! It was my fault. I did not give my kids the part that a parent is responsible for.

God gives us, as parents, certain authority – not just **_over_** our children but **_for_** our children. With that authority, as a parent, comes a certain responsibility. The authority is for parents to take charge and guide, direct, correct, and train them as we see fit. Then we, as parents, also have the responsibility to teach, protect, provide for, love them, help them find their bent, their place, and their niche in this life.

The problem is our stubborn refusal to follow the instructions in His Manual. Oh, Yes! He has given us an Instruction Manual for this life. Though it may not call each child by name or list each problem, it is the Manual for life. It may not list their personality traits one by one, yet it is full of principles and guidelines for rearing children, living it before them, good counsel and practical walking as their parents. It's called the Bible.

Even if it doesn't come with a written blow-by-blow, day-by-day schedule of what to do next, we are still without excuse because we have direct access to the Author of the Book and the Creator of the Universe for specific instructions. Most of us have heard of it but many of us just flat out think it isn't for us. It's a little bit like putting a complicated toy together at Christmas time. The instructions and directions and all parts come with the toy. Somehow, we don't think we need the instruction manual. I mean after all, you have all of the parts, right? How difficult can it be? People all over the world do this every day.

You know when we start thinking about the instructions? When we've made a mess of putting the thing together and not only are there left over parts but you stand there watching the stuffing, springs, and screws begin to pop out all over the place. It looked great at first, but under pressure and over time, it just wasn't right.

We start thinking about the instructions for life when we experience a fullness inside of our hearts or a great emptiness. When we think we're going to burst or explode or when there seems to be nothing left to fill that emptiness, that void, Extremes we don't know how to deal with because we didn't take the time to read, study, and follow the Instruction Manual. We didn't read His love letters to His Wayward and His Would Be or Could Be children. The Bible. Our Operational Manual. The Instruction Manual for Life.

Real life is much more complicated than any man made toy. We finally get the message when the toy is a mess. Some of us finally get the message for our lives when we lie bleeding, with gaping near mortal wounds, shattered on the floor, and splattered on the walls. Sometimes we're like heaps of ashes on the floor, our hearts and minds so messed up that thinking is almost impossible. We can barely function. And still, Our Loving, Gracious, Forgiving God, Our Heavenly Father stands there with arms wide open. He'll take us in our weak and bloody state. He still extends His love letters, the Instruction Manual to us. He still wants us.

I travelled many years with my mother as a migrant worker. I saw way too much way too soon. The lifestyles some of the people led were quite sad. From homosexuality to multiple wives and girlfriends, live-in boyfriends, outside girlfriends, petty theft, grand theft, murder, attempted murder, rape, incest, physical, mental and emotional abuse, neglect, abandonment, and drug and alcohol abuse – you name it, I have probably seen it. Still, I kept dreaming of something different. It was only when I began to experience the devastation first hand that I began to lose hope.

Proverbs 13:12 Hope delayed or taken away leaves a person empty and devoid of anything except futility for the future. Habakkuk 2:2-3 talks about the vision, the dream – though it tarries, it takes a while, wait for it! God not only restored some of my dreams but He gave me good and proper dreams then began fulfilling them! After all this time and all of that stuff. He still gives and fulfills dreams.

My desire is to pass some hope on to you. Within the walls of your heart, your mind, your soul, God has planted something wonderful. Be willing to break out of the prison that satan has surrounded you with. Go for it! Run home to Jesus and His merciful freedom. His Word brings the message that the prison doors are open (Isaiah 61). All you need to do is walk out of there into His Arms. Dare to do it and watch God work for you.

Freedom begins, ultimately in your mind. So does the bondage of our lives. Romans 12:1-2 says: "I beseech you therefore, brethren, by the mercies of God, that ye present your bodies a living sacrifice, holy, acceptable unto God, which is your reasonable service. AND BE NOT CONFORMED TO THIS WORLD: BUT BE YE TRANSFORMED BY THE RENEWING OF YOUR MIND, THAT YE MAY PROVE WHAT IS THAT GOOD AND ACCEPTABLE, AND PERFECT WILL OF GOD." The way to begin transforming your mind is to read, study, and devour the Word of God. Starting *NOW!*

When the Stuff is Too Thick

If you don't know Jesus as Lord and Savior, this would be a really good time to do that. Would you allow me to introduce you to My Very Best Friend, My Ultimate Love, My Prince of Peace, My Peace in the Midst of Every Storm, My Strong Provider, My Defender, My Attorney, My God, My Lord. His Name is Jesus Christ. He lived, suffered, and died for you. His resurrection assures salvation and keeping power for all who believe and accept Him as Lord and Savior. Acts 16:31 If you believe… Romans 6:8-10 He died for all… Romans 10:9-10 Confession and salvation…He wants you but He still allows free will, choice. He has so much to offer. More than you could ever imagine. Bottom line, it is still your decision. The buck stops here.

I can't tell God how to run His business and I wouldn't assume any such wisdom for being able to. By a similar principle, I will not try to tell you how to run your life. I only know that sometimes, we as humans are so caught up, involved in, wrapped up, tied up, tangled up in our affairs, that we find our thoughts and ability to reason, muddled. Sometimes, we're too close to the flames or the fire to really be able to make good decisions based on (oftentimes) the things that we know are right to do. The thickness of things prove to be too great, too much for us to see clearly. We're in the middle of the forest so we can't see all of the trees or the end of the path. We're in the heaviest part of the fog.

That's why it is so important to stay close to the God Who knows all things – Past, Present, and Future. Not only does He know what's happening where I am right now but He also knows what's happening thousands of miles away at the same time. He knows the things that may affect me and others. He has all of that within His View. He sees, He knows, He understands. It is important for me to stay close so that I can hear and understand because He still speaks to His children.

He advises, counsels, urges, prompts by His Holy Spirit. This is ever so important, vital. For in times of adversity, confusion, muddled thoughts, painful situations, overwhelming circumstances; when things are happening that just don't make sense, when I'm unsure – I need to be still, get quiet, listen. For I need to hear from Him Who Knows all Things!

So, Where Does the Fault Lie? Who is to Blame?

Whether it is a child out of control, away from God, a loved one sick and perhaps dying, a financial situation that just won't go away, our own health issues, a straying church member, a strained relationship, an estranged family member, a nasty habit that has become sin – it doesn't matter what it is. What matters is how we handle it right now. It can't be blamed on our past, our ignorance, our inability. The thing that really matters is what we do from this point on.

How eager are we to gird up the loins of our minds and begin to fix the messes we've made? My God, how long will we halt between two opinions? How long will we stand and blame our past for what we continue doing and know it's wrong? How long will we try to keep blaming Mom, Dad, Uncle Joe, Aunt Lyddi, Cousin Poppy twice removed? How long will we continue to blame the next door neighbor? The bully down the street? The teacher from 4th grade? The History Professor? The Pastor from 6 churches ago? The boss from the first job? The mortgage lender? The electric company? The car dealer? The restaurant chain? The ex-boyfriend? Ex-wife? Ex-husband? The molesting cousin? Step-mother, step-father? God handles them.

We have become a society which casts blame. We choose to blame somebody else for everything we do that does not turn out the way we wanted it to. When I took ownership and responsibility for my wrongdoing, I confessed it and then decided to forsake it. I began to walk in a freedom that I can't even explain. I had never known anything like it. I'm not talking just an emotional high. They tend to wear off over time. I'm talking about a life changing event. I didn't even know such a thing existed.

It didn't let my parents off the hook for what they did or did not do for me. It didn't let my abusers off the hook for injuring me. It didn't let me off the hook for not providing for and protecting my girls. It helped me to face those things without condemnation. Yes, those things happened. Yes, they were wrong but Jesus has taken the punishment for them all and I am free to walk in that freedom. I can walk in holiness, sanctification, clean and not weighted down. If I need to talk about it, I can do it and not wallow in self-pity anymore. I can speak life to someone else who may be right where I was and tell them that they can come out of prison!

It started me on a journey of agreeing with God. A path of learning the value that God places on each individual – even the ones who hurt me, injured me, cheated me, damaged me! It allowed me to see the infinite value God has placed on each individual and how quickly He forgives us when we ask. He forgives. He provides the help we need for restoration. Sometimes He restores just because it gives Him pleasure.

Talk about taking a load off of our shoulders! A load we were never designed to carry in this life. Whew! I know it did for me.

Imagine carrying a whole other person around on your back, then realizing all you have to do is shake them off? Drop the load because it isn't your load anymore. Believe me, Beloved, You can do this.

Made in USA - Crawfordsville, IN
37759_9781534991101
04.27.2020 0602